# The Purple Book

## What to Do When You're Nervous

by
William Anthony

Minneapolis, Minnesota

**Credits**

Cover and throughout - Ekaterina Kapranova, Beatriz Gascon J. 4 - NLshop. 7 - S-Victoria, Nikolaeva, Marti Bug Catcher, Ken StockPhoto. 9 -Albina Makarowa. 10 - Kovalov Anatolii, kondratya, Tetiana Rostopira. 14 -Ign, fotoslaz. 16 - Choreograph.  21 - runLenarun, metrometro. 22 - NLshop. Additional illustrations by Danielle Webster-Jones. All images courtesy of Shutterstock.com. With thanks to Getty Images, Thinkstock Photo and iStockphoto.

Library of Congress Cataloging-in-Publication Data is available at www.loc.gov or upon request from the publisher.

ISBN: 978-1-64747-579-6 (hardcover)
ISBN: 978-1-64747-584-0 (paperback)
ISBN: 978-1-64747-589-5 (ebook)

© 2022 Booklife Publishing

This edition is published by arrangement with Booklife Publishing.

North American adaptations © 2022 Bearport Publishing Company. All rights reserved. No part of this publication may be reproduced in whole or in part, stored in any retrieval system, or transmitted in any form or by any means, electronic, mechanical, photocopying, recording, or otherwise, without written permission from the publisher.

For more information, write to Bearport Publishing, 5357 Penn Avenue South, Minneapolis, MN 55419.

For more
The Purple Book activities:

1. Go to **www.factsurfer.com**

2. Enter **"Purple Book"** into the search box.

3. Click on the cover of this book to see a list of activities.

# CONTENTS

Imagine a Rainbow . . . . . . . . . . . . . . . . . . . 4

Road Trip . . . . . . . . . . . . . . . . . . . . . . . . . . 6

The Breathing Star . . . . . . . . . . . . . . . . . 8

Little Lotus . . . . . . . . . . . . . . . . . . . . . . 10

Peaceful Planet . . . . . . . . . . . . . . . . . . 12

The Worry Well . . . . . . . . . . . . . . . . . . 14

Slip into Sleep . . . . . . . . . . . . . . . . . . . 16

Super You . . . . . . . . . . . . . . . . . . . . . . . 18

Little Ideas . . . . . . . . . . . . . . . . . . . . . . 20

Feeling Better? . . . . . . . . . . . . . . . . . . 22

Glossary . . . . . . . . . . . . . . . . . . . . . . . . 24

Index . . . . . . . . . . . . . . . . . . . . . . . . . . . 24

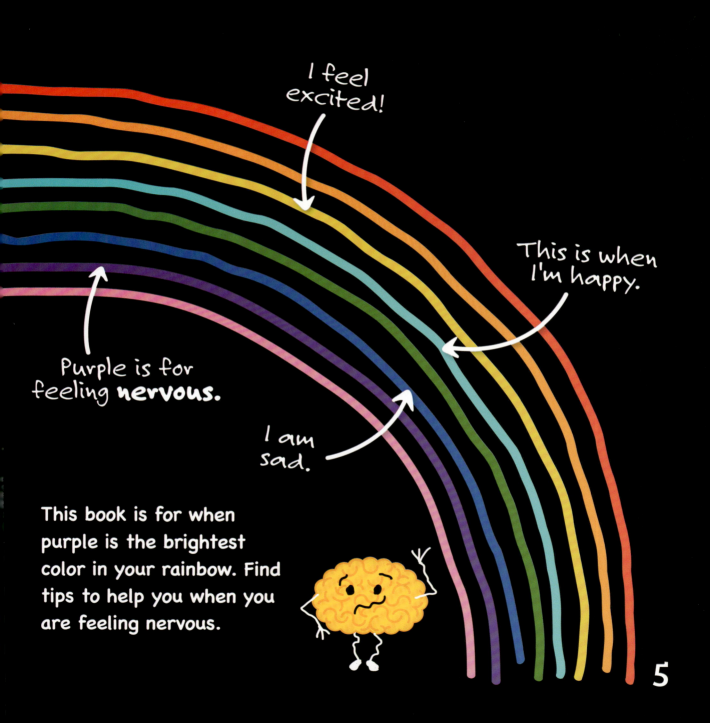

# ROAD TRIP

Finding the right word to describe how you are feeling can be hard. If nervous isn't it, take a road trip around this map.

Look for signs on the map that describe how you are feeling. You can use them when you are talking to someone (or point to them if you don't feel like talking).

## TOP TIP!

Ask an adult if you don't know what a word means. They can describe what each **emotion** feels like.

# THE BREATHING STAR

If we get nervous really fast, we might start to **panic**. When we panic, our hearts start pounding and we breathe much faster.

Get your breathing under control with the breathing star. Trace the outline of the star with your finger. As your finger moves toward one of the points, breathe in. When you reach the point, hold your breath for two seconds. As you trace the next side, breathe out.

Worries can make it hard to think clearly.

**Yoga** is exercise that can help us relax so we can think more clearly. In yoga, we pay attention to our breathing and let our worries leave our bodies.

Try some yoga. Follow the steps on the next page.

10

## STEP 1:
Sit somewhere comfortable with your legs in front of you.

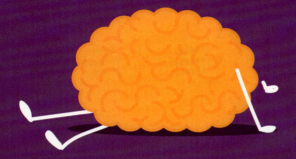

## STEP 2:
Cross your legs.

## STEP 3:
Bring your hands to your knees and hold them like this.

## STEP 4:
Relax your shoulders, close your eyes, and take some deep breaths.

# PEACEFUL PLANET

Imagining a **peaceful** place can help us relax when we feel nervous.

> Use the questions on the next page to help you create a peaceful planet. You could draw your planet to help you remember it.

Close your eyes and explore your planet. Focus on what you can see, hear, and smell.

> Visit your peaceful planet whenever you need to relax.

**TOP TIP!**
You could visit your peaceful planet when you are doing yoga!

12

# THE WORRY WELL

Talking can be a good way to let go of our worries. But sometimes it can seem too hard to talk to another person.

Meet the worry well. You can tell it everything that is bothering you.

Talking to the worry well first may make it easier to share your feelings with someone else.

**TOP TIP!**

Take the worry well to a quiet room away from other people.

# SLIP INTO SLEEP

Falling asleep can be hard when you are nervous.

Giving your mind something relaxing to think about is the perfect way to help you slip into sleep.

Use your senses to follow along with the steps on the next page. When you get to the last one, you may find it easier to fall asleep.

**TOP TIP!** Keep a night-light on to help you with this activity.

Try to find...

2) things you can
SEE

1) things you can
FEEL

3) things you can
HEAR

4) things you can
SMELL

5) a place in the world that makes you
VERY HAPPY

Finally, try to picture...

17

# SUPER YOU

Sometimes we get upset, act scared, or say something we don't mean. When we've calmed down, we might feel bad about ourselves. This is okay!

> When we feel like this, it is important to remember how super we are!

Get a trusted adult or friend and follow the steps on the next page together.

## STEP 1:
Grab some pencils and paper.

## STEP 2:
Write something you are good at or why people like you. Don't let the other person see!

## STEP 3:
Now, ask the other person to do the same thing about you.

## STEP 4:
When you are both finished, show each other what makes you so super!

# LITTLE IDEAS

There are lots of little tips and tricks you can use when you feel nervous.

## GO FOR A WALK

Sometimes it helps to walk away from something that is making you nervous.

## CLOSE YOUR EYES

Close your eyes and try to picture everything in the room that is purple. This will help you think about something else.

# NERVOUS NOTES

Keep a **diary** of what makes you feel most nervous. Then, you can avoid these things or find a way to deal with them.

## STRETCH

Gently rolling your neck and shoulders can help relax your body.

## CALM KIT

Fill a box with things that calm you down. You can put in music, things to draw with, a book, and anything that makes you happy.

# FEELING BETTER?

Which tip worked best for you? Why do you think that is?

If you feel calmer, now is a good time to think about what made you feel nervous and why. How might you handle things the next time you feel nervous?

Remember, you are like everyone else. We all have colorful minds.

Every feeling you have is important!
This book will still be here

# whenever

you need it.

23

# GLOSSARY

**diary** a book in which you write down your thoughts and experiences

**emotion** a strong feeling, such as love, anger, joy, sadness, or fear

**nervous** worried or afraid about what might happen

**panic** very strong fear that makes it hard to think clearly

**peaceful** quiet and calm

**relax** to stop feeling nervous or worried

**yoga** a set of exercises for your mind and body

# INDEX

breathing 8–11
diary 21
panic 8–9
relaxing 9–12, 16

senses 16
sleep 4, 16
talking 6, 14–15
yoga 10–12